For Snicklefritz

-Rebecca Atanassova

Popsicle Publishing
P.O. Box 2588 Alexandria, V822301
www.popsiclepublishing.com
Copyright @ 2023 Rebecca Atanassova
All rights reserved.
ISBN:978-1-960746-05-4

You may be silly, and run around willy-nilly.
But that's why I love you, Snicklefritz.

You may be giddy, and play dress up with kitty.
But that's why I love you, Snicklefritz.

You may parade through,
And make a hullabaloo!
But that's why I love you, Snicklefritz.

You may be chatty on the phone with Aunt Hattie.
But that's why I love you, Snicklefritz.

You may be upsy-daisy,
And make me kinda crazy!
But that's why I love you, Snicklefritz.

You may be sleepy, and start to feel weepy,
You may be a grouch, and go pout on the couch.
But I still love you, Snicklefritz.

You may be all zany,
When outside it's rainy.
You may spoil your clothes, from your head to your toes.
But that's why I love you, Snicklefritz.

You may be loony,
With your dinner-time spoony.
But that's why I love you, Snicklefritz.

You may make a blooper,
But you're still super duper.
You may act all wild,
But you still are my child.
I will ALWAYS love you, Snicklefritz.

Made in the USA
Las Vegas, NV
05 April 2024